First published in Great Britain in 2000 by Macdonald Young Books

Macdonald Young Books,
an imprint of Wayland Publishers Ltd
61 Western Road
Hove
East Sussex
BN3 1JD

Text © Pat Thomas 2000
Illustrations © Lesley Harker 2000
Volume © Macdonald Young Books 2000

Editor: Lisa Edwards
Concept design: Kate Buxton
Book designer: Jean Wheeler

A CIP catalogue for this book is available from the British Library

Printed and bound in Portugal by Edições ASA

ISBN 0 7500 2887 4

Find Macdonald Young Books on the Internet
at http://www.myb.co.uk

Stop Picking on Me

A FIRST LOOK AT BULLYING

PAT THOMAS
ILLUSTRATED BY LESLEY HARKER

MACDONALD YOUNG BOOKS

Some of these children are bullies.
Can you tell which ones?

Bullies look just like everyone else but
they don't act like everyone else.

Bullies enjoy hurting other people and
making them do what they say.

The only way they know how to get
what they want is by being cruel.

Bullies don't always hurt your body, they can hurt your feelings as well. A bully can make you feel like it's your fault that they are picking on you, even though this isn't true.

What about you?

Do you know anyone who is a bully?
What sort of things do they do?

Anyone can be a bully.
It could be a boy or a girl,
a person on their own or
in a gang.

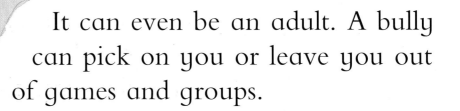

It can even be an adult. A bully
can pick on you or leave you out
of games and groups.

At some time in their lives, most people have hurt someone else, without meaning to, by acting like a bully. But some people act this way all the time.

Bullies never have a good reason for hurting other people. Often they pick on anyone who they think is different from them.

Some bullies pick on people who are a different size from them or whose skin is a different colour. Some bullies will even pick on you because of the clothes you are wearing.

Anyone who acts like a bully has probably
been bullied themselves, sometimes by
other children.

Sometimes their parents, or other adults, may have been cruel to them. This is very sad, but it is never a good reason for being unkind to others.

Bullies don't like themselves very
much. This makes it hard for
them to like other people
and treat them well.

The only way bullies can like themselves is to pick on others. Doing this makes them feel more powerful.

We all need to feel loved. That is why being bullied hurts so much. When someone is bullying you, it can make you feel scared or angry, miserable or hurt.

You may not want to sleep or when you do sleep you may have nightmares. You may not feel like eating or going to school anymore.

What about you?

Everyone feels differently about being bullied.
Have you ever been bullied?
How did it make you feel?

You don't deserve to be bullied.
Nobody does.

One of the hardest
things to learn is how to
deal with a bully without becoming
a bully yourself. Hitting back or being
cruel usually only makes the problem worse.

What about you?

What sort of things do you do when someone bullies you? Can you think of any different ways to deal with a bully?

A good way to stop bullying is
to talk to someone about it.
This can be a parent
or a teacher or any
grown-up you feel
comfortable with.

You may not want
to talk to anyone
about it, but
you should.

All bullies hope that their victims won't tell
on them. Keeping it to yourself lets a bully
know that it's alright to go on hurting you.

Another way to stop bullies is to let the people who love you help. Other people's love can help you feel good about yourself and reassure you that it's not your fault if you are bullied.

Bullies only pick on people they know
they can hurt. Feeling good about
yourself and liking yourself is probably
the best way to stop them.

Also, when you feel good about yourself
you do not need to bully others
to get what you want.

That's important to remember because
the fewer bullies there are in our world, the
better place it will be for all of us to live in.

HOW TO USE THIS BOOK

A bullied child will have many powerful feelings – don't let these panic or overwhelm you. A bullied child needs unconditional love first and foremost. If you try to make it 'better' – for instance make your child less unhappy, less angry or less scared – you are not accepting your child's feelings. You can make your child more confident by giving them the freedom to express their feelings.

When your child is being bullied it can sometimes bring up powerful memories of being bullied yourself. When your child is a victim, it makes you a victim too and this is very frightening for many adults. Try not to work unresolved feelings out through your child. Don't make your child fight the bully you wish you had fought or say what you wish you had said.

Children learn how to behave at home. If your child is involved in bullying others it is a good time to look objectively at the way they are being treated at home and the way various family members interact with each other.

Schools are in a powerful position to stamp out bullying. Those schools with a zero tolerance for bullying generally have the lowest rates of bullying behaviour among students. The 'bully box', where children can report bullying anonymously, should be a part of every school.

Individual classes can also help to promote discussion about bullying. A useful way to do this is through role play. Children in the class should be given the opportunity through short improvisations to act out both the role of the bully and the bullied in front of the class. Group discussion can then take place about how it feels to be bullied, how best to cope with bullying and what to do if you are being bullied.

BOOKS TO READ

For Adults

Freedom From Bullying
Mildred Masheder (Green Print, 1998)
Available from 75 Belsize Lane, London NW3 5AU.
Teaching packs also available.

Your Child and Bullying
Jenny Alexander (Element, 1998)

For Children

How Do I Feel About Bullies and Gangs?
Julie Johnson (Franklin Watts, 1996)

I Feel Bullied
Jen Green/Mike Gordon (Wayland, 1999)

What Do We Think About Bullying?
Jillian Powell (Wayland, 1998)

USEFUL CONTACTS

Anti-Bullying Campaign
185 Tower Bridge Road
London SE1 2UF
0171-378-1446
*Support service for parents of bullied children, offering counselling
and advice. Produces information packs for parents and schools.*

Childline
Freepost 1111
London N1 0BR
0800-111111
*Children can phone any time of the day to talk to someone
about bullying. All calls are free.*

Kidscape
2 Grosvenor Gardens
London SW1W 0DH
0171-730-330
*Registered charity which provides books, videos, teaching packs
and leaflets on how to deal with bullying. Parents Bullying
Helpline operates on Mondays and Wednesdays 9am – 5pm.
Send SAE for free 20-page booklet,* Stop Bullying.

NSPCC
National Society for the Prevention of Cruelty to
Children
67 Saffron Hill
London EC1N 8RS
0171-242-1626